HELP!

MY FLESH NEEDS
DISCIPLINE

DR. CREFLO A. DOLLAR

Help! My Flesh Needs Discipline
ISBN 1-88507-216-3
Copyright © 1998, 2005 by Dr. Creflo A. Dollar

Published by:
Creflo Dollar Ministries
P.O. Box 490124
College Park, GA 30349

Contents

Introduction

Lasciviousness, or "a lack of restraint or control," over one's life is a tool used by the Devil to distract Believers and take their focus off of the Word of God. When you sow to the flesh, you position yourself to experience the consequences of your behavior (Galatians 6:8).

You are a spirit who possesses a soul (the place where your mind, will and emotions reside)—both of which are housed in a body. God never designed for your physical man to be in control of everything. Instead, He intended for you to develop your *spirit man* to operate in line with His Word so that you may live a life that is rich in blessings. That is why the anointing of discipline has been made available to you. When employed, it counteracts the worldly temptation to engage in activities and practices that transgress the Word of God.

If you have allowed your life to get out of control, this book will give you insight as to why it is necessary for you to modify your behavior. It will require a change on your part to experience an abundance of God's blessings. My prayer is that the information contained in these pages will renew your mind to the way God wants you to live. First Corinthians 14:40 says, *"Let all things be done decently and in order."* Living a life of decency and order requires you to operate in the anointing of discipline.

CHAPTER ONE

Your Expected End

Have you ever wondered how your life will turn out? Many people hope good things will happen to them. They want to live prosperous, healthy lives filled with harmonious relationships. But when it comes right down to it, they don't know what to expect.

That should not, however, be the case for a Believer. According to Scripture, you can have "an expected end." God said so through the Prophet Jeremiah: *"For I know the thoughts that I think toward you, saith the Lord, thoughts of peace, and not of evil, to give you an expected end"* (Jeremiah 29:11).

What does the Word of God mean by an "expected end"? First, it describes the spiritual principle that you tend to receive what you expect. The result you expect is the one you're most likely to receive. That's why the ways in which you think, talk and act are such powerful influences on your quality of life. Faith and expectation are closely related. Second, your expected end is the outcome God desires for you. The Word clearly states that His will is for you to be healed and to walk in abundance and freedom from bondage of any kind.

In these last days, more Believers than ever before are beginning to employ the faith to make that kind of life possible. More and more are beginning to experience the benefits of the burden-removing, yoke-destroying power of the anointing (Isaiah 10:27).

The bad news is that Satan will surely make a desperate attempt to keep as many of us as possible from fully experiencing these new dimensions of power and freedom. The devil knows that his time is short. You can be sure that he's planning some type of deception designed to keep you from seeing your expected end.

I'm convinced that Satan is trying to use slothfulness as a weapon to short-circuit the power of God in your life.

Webster's Dictionary defines *slothfulness* as "an aversion to work or exertion; laziness; sluggishness." We don't hear the word "slothfulness" used much anymore because this Old English word has been replaced by more modern words. However, I believe that the real reason lies in the fact that we're living in a culture in which slothfulness has become so common that most people think it is normal.

If you, as a Believer, are going to experience the wonderful fullness of God's expected end for your life, you must go against the tide of this present age and deal with slothfulness. If you're bold enough to do so, you'll experience more blessings and more accomplishments than you have ever dreamed possible.

Crowning the Flesh King

As I began to consider what the Lord had revealed to me concerning the enemy's weapon of slothfulness in these last days, a picture came into my mind. It was a contrast between a new Believer and one who has gradually slipped into the grip of slothfulness.

If you are like most Christians, immediately after being born again you found that you were zealous for God. You were in church every time the doors were open. If someone was hosting a Bible study, you were there. Once you heard the truth from the Word concerning tithing, that was all you needed. God received His 10 percent right away, come hell or high water! As for a regular quiet time? You had better believe it! When your alarm went off an hour earlier than usual, you jumped out of bed.

Now, instead of being in church at every opportunity, you find it easy to miss services, telling yourself you'll get the tapes instead, but never do. Without realizing it, you go weeks at a stretch without ever sitting under the anointing of the ministry of the Holy Spirit. You also find less and less time for the Word, telling yourself that because you're a mature Christian now, you don't need as much study time as you did in the beginning. Your morning quiet time has also fallen by the wayside. At some point, the snooze button became your closest friend; although you keep meaning to get up and pray, you never seem to manage to do so.

Somewhere along the line, you stop tithing and giving offerings. When you get your year-end giving report from the church, you become shocked and embarrassed. You discover your giving fell far short of the 10 percent the Word of God sets as the minimum standard for qualifying to receive the blessings of God that come through tithing.

What happened to the fire? What happened to the zeal? Where did the commitment go? The hard, cold truth is that most Believers have become victims of slothfulness. In other words, they have crowned their flesh king over their lives. How does such a thing happen? Well, it doesn't happen overnight. It's gradual and it's primarily the result of a lack of discipline.

I know for a lot of supposedly "spiritual" people, discipline is a dirty word. In a time of trial and adversity, they are quick to say, "Oh yes, God will deliver me. He will do it. Yes, amen!" But the unpleasant reality is that the answer will never come, because they lack the personal discipline necessary to operate in God's system. To see the fullness of God's promises, you *must* operate according to His standards. A slothful man simply won't do that. Don't get offended. Stay with me and allow me to show you the progression of how a promise of God can manifest in your life and how slothfulness can short-circuit that progression.

A Natural Progression

Have you ever come across a promise in God's Word and become excited about it? That surge of excitement is what I call "desire." You are excited by the thought of realizing that promise. But true delight comes in seeing that promise becoming a reality in your life.

Many Believers get to the desire stage. They see a promise of healing or abundance in the Word, and they want it. Sadly, that's where most people stop. They never move past their desires. Why is that? Because the next stage calls for *discipline*. And as I have stated previously, the attribute of discipline is very rare among Christians today. With discipline, you'll ultimately see that promise become a reality. That's when you move into the stage called "delight."

Desire. Discipline. Delight. That's the sequence you must follow if you want to experience God's best for your life. And what is discipline's worst enemy? Slothfulness.

Discipline is defined as "a state of order based on submission to rules and authority." I like this definition. We have spiritual authority through God and His Word. He has put certain rules, or spiritual principles, in place in the universe. To be spiritually disciplined is to submit your life to the spiritual principles of faith.

Another definition of *discipline* is "to train or drill by instruction." This also sheds some light on the subject. In the military, to *drill* means to "repeatedly work on something until it becomes second nature." Does that sound like hard work? It is. But it's absolutely necessary if you want to get to the delight stage. The basic things of God—such as prayer, Bible study, sharing your faith, thinking right and talking right—must become second nature to you if you want to experience the delight of seeing God's wonderful promises made manifest in your life. Something becomes second nature only with consistent, methodical repetition.

Discipline is vital to getting to the delight stage. That's why so few Believers are living "delight-full" lives. Of course, discipline is rarely fun—especially in the beginning. If you have ever resolved to get up an hour early to spend time with God, you know what I'm talking about. If you *did* manage to drag yourself out of bed the first day, it probably took a lot of effort. The same was probably true for the second and the third day.

I once read a study that said it takes six weeks of consistent behavior to create a firm habit. Most people quit long before they reach that point. Slothfulness comes in and moves discipline out of the way. For example, if you've ever decided to embark on a campaign of serious exercise after a long period of idleness, you can relate to what I'm saying. You see a picture of a slim and trim individual in a magazine and say, "Hey, that could be me!" At that point, you have desire; next comes the discipline. You go to the gym and use the exercise equipment with great zeal. The following day, however, you're sore from head to toe. Even your hair hurts. Muscles you didn't even know you had are sore! At that point, slothfulness is going to do its best to keep you from getting disciplined about your workouts. Either you're going to keep working out each day until it becomes a regular part of your daily routine, much like brushing your teeth or taking a shower, or you're going to quit because it's too hard.

That is the point that determines whether you experience delight or defeat. The same is true concerning spiritual matters. Jesus said, *"...If ye continue in my word, then are ye my disciples indeed; and ye shall know the truth, and the truth shall make you free"* (John 8:31-32). According to Jesus, it is only when we continue in His Word (remaining disciplined) that we come to know truth and find freedom.

We've casually quoted John 8:32 for years: "The truth will make you free." However, many have taken Jesus' words out of context. He said, *"...If you continue in my word..."* (verse 31). In other words, the truth that we know and *consistently* employ in our lives makes us His disciples, or His disciplined ones. Then, and *only* then, will we be free.

I know many drug addicts who know the truth about their addiction, but they are not free of it. Why aren't they? They have neither begun nor continued in the Word. I'm acquainted with people who know the Word better than I do, yet they don't *do* any of it. They do not experience delight or freedom, because they don't continue in the Word.

If, on the other hand, a person pushes through the soreness of the first few days of a new "spiritual" workout program and keeps on hitting the "gym" with consistency, what began as an unpleasant chore will become an anticipated delight. Instead of dreading his spiritual development, he begins to look forward to it. Before long, results will begin to show in the form of toned muscles, weight loss, greater energy levels and increased strength. Through discipline, desire becomes delight.

God never designed your flesh to be in control. He designed a system in which your born-again spirit—that part of you made alive by the life of God Himself—is in the driver's seat. Your spirit is supposed to determine the direction of your life. Still, most Believers let their flesh call the shots. The flesh says, "Sleep a little longer. You don't need to get up and spend time with God. You need your rest." King Flesh has spoken!

Yes, your flesh will talk to you. It will talk to you when it's raining on Sunday morning and it's time to get ready for church. It will talk to you when the offering plate passes by. It will talk to you when someone offends you. It will talk to you when sexual temptation presents itself.

Believers who, through neglect or slothfulness, crown their flesh king, never see their visions, or God-given dreams, come to fruition. The marvelous promises of God never manifest, because they lack the vital quality of discipline.

To discover how to cultivate that quality, read on.

CHAPTER TWO

Discipline
and the Anointing

What does the anointing—the burden-removing, yoke-destroying power of God—have to do with the subject of discipline? Plenty. When you fail to discipline yourself in the natural, that failure ultimately translates into failure in spiritual things.

You can't hear from God if you lack the discipline to sit still during church service to listen to the Word that is being ministered. How are you going to grow as a Christian if you can't even make yourself go to church? Neither can you experience the riches of God's abundance without the discipline to give God your tithe (10 percent of your gross income). It's clear; failure to discipline yourself in one simple, natural area can mean failure in another.

I had to face that reality personally. If I let my body go, ate whatever I felt like eating and basically exercised no control over my physical condition, it would ultimately impact me spiritually. How could I pastor a church if my flesh was calling the shots in other areas of my life? I couldn't. If my spirit man were not in control over natural things like my appetite, it wouldn't be in control in spiritual matters either.

Discipline. It's a hard word, but it's a word very much tied to the anointing. This is a truth that is stated very plainly in Galatians 6:7-8: *"Be not deceived; God is not mocked: for whatsoever a man soweth, that shall he also reap. For he that soweth to his flesh shall of the flesh reap corruption; but he that soweth to the Spirit shall of the Spirit reap life everlasting."* The first thing I want you to notice here is that God said, *"Be not deceived...."* That means this is an area in which it is easy to get into deception. The next thing that is important to note is that *"...God is not mocked.*" Do you know what the word *mock* means? It means, "to make a fool of." You can't fool God, and you certainly can't make a fool of Him.

The Word of God gets down to the heart of the matter. It says, "*...for whatsoever a man soweth, that shall he also reap.*" This phrase is familiar to most of us. We've heard it hundreds of times. But very few of us have thought much about the implications of the very next sentence: "*For he that soweth to his flesh shall of the flesh reap corruption; but he that soweth to the Spirit shall of the Spirit reap life everlasting.*"

What does it mean to sow to your flesh? It means to keep pleasing your flesh. You let your flesh tell you to stay in bed a little longer. Sowing to the Spirit would involve hauling yourself out of bed to spend time with God. You sow to your flesh when you focus your eyes and ears on unclean things that appear on television or in magazines. You sow to the Spirit when you give your eyes and ears over to the teaching of the Word. What does this passage of Scripture say we can expect if we sow to the flesh? A harvest of corruption, or death.

Many Christians blame the devil for the negative things they experience in their lives. However, the reality is that they are simply reaping a harvest of corruption because they've consistently sown to their flesh instead of sowing to the Spirit. For example, if you let the cravings of your flesh determine what you're going to eat (i.e., a steady diet of saturated fat, processed sugar, additives and preservatives), then, over the course of your lifetime, you shouldn't be shocked to hear your doctor give you a bad report.

If you sow to the flesh, you will reap corruption. It's not just true where food is concerned. It's true of every appetite your flesh can create, including a sexual appetite, an appetite for leisure and rest, an appetite for comfort or the appetite for the praises of men. Let one or more of these appetites rule your life, and you can rest assured that you will reap a harvest you won't like. Do not be deceived. God can't be made a fool of, and King Flesh is a cruel tyrant.

Listen to Your Flesh and Do the Opposite

When your flesh tries to give orders, do the opposite of what it wants. Keep it under subjection. That is exactly what Paul said he did: "*...But I keep under my body, and bring it into subjection: lest that by any means, when I have preached to others, I myself should be a castaway*" (1 Corinthians 9:27).

Paul knew what too few Christians know today: failure to keep your flesh on a tight leash ultimately leads to spiritual disaster. Even Paul knew that he would become a spiritual castaway if he didn't keep his body under subjection. A reason why this is so important is that God cannot direct a man through his flesh. God is a Spirit and chooses to direct you only through your spirit. Proverbs 20:27 says, *"The spirit of man is the candle of the Lord, searching all the inward parts of the belly."*

As with a candle, your way through life is lit as your born-again spirit communes with and receives direction from the Holy Spirit. When you give your flesh too much authority, you cut yourself off from God's life-giving, life-saving direction. For example, I don't know how many times I've heard someone say, "Sometimes I just don't feel like praising the Lord when everyone else is singing." What this person is really saying is that King Flesh doesn't want to praise God. At that moment, the flesh is dominant. At this time, a choice must be made. The person can sow to his flesh, or he can sow to the Spirit and praise God, whether his flesh feels like it or not!

"But isn't that being phony or hypocritical?" you may ask. Not at all! Your born-again spirit wants to praise and please God and commune with Him. Regrettably, when your flesh is highly developed, you can't hear or sense the desire of your spirit. Look at what Galatians 5:16-17 has to say concerning this subject: *"This I say then, Walk in the Spirit, and ye shall not fulfil the lust of the flesh. For the flesh lusteth against the Spirit, and the Spirit against the flesh: and these are contrary the one to the other: so that ye cannot do the things that ye would."*

Did you catch that? The desires of your spirit and the desires of your flesh are pulling in opposite directions. Look at that same passage of Scripture using the *New American Standard Bible* translation: *"But I say, walk by the Spirit, and you will not carry out the desire of the flesh. For the flesh sets its desire against the Spirit, and the Spirit against the flesh; for these are in opposition to one another, so that you may not do the things that you please."* The first part of this passage contains a wonderful promise: *"Walk by the Spirit, and you will not carry out the desire of the flesh."* In other words, sow to the Spirit, and you will reap a harvest of abundant life!

You sow to the Spirit when you do those things that your born-again spirit desires, which are the same things the Spirit of God desires. And what does the Holy Spirit desire? He desires the things that are in the Word, because He and the Word are in agreement!

Now, let's look at Galatians 6:9 since it gives us an important key to walking in the anointing of discipline: *"And let us not be weary in well doing: for in due season we shall reap, if we faint not.*" Here, the condition for reaping a harvest of life is that we must "faint not." The word *faint* means, "to give up, cave in or quit." All too often, quitting is the story with many Believers.

I've seen the most committed church members quit when weariness sets in. Consequently, they never see their due season of harvest. Why? Their "package" of blessing eventually arrives through God's angelic delivery service after being temporarily delayed by demonic resistance in the spiritual realm; however, when the manifestation of His blessing comes, there is no one there to sign for it. Often, a Believer's blessing is undeliverable, because the recipient gave up before his or her due season arrived.

No Believer can receive God's best in life by giving up, caving in or quitting. When you start quitting in natural things, you'll eventually start quitting in spiritual things as well. For example, if you'll quit on your marital relationship, you'll give up on your relationship with God. If you're unfaithful to your spouse, you'll be unfaithful to Jesus.

I've had people tell me, "Brother Dollar, if I become a millionaire, I'll give the church everything it needs." I know they're lying, because if they don't tithe from their minimum-wage income, they won't give the tithe on a million dollars. Those who are unfaithful in the little things will never be faithful in the big ones (Luke 16:10).

What makes a person weary? According to Hebrews 12:1, it is weight: "*Wherefore seeing we also are compassed about with so great a cloud of witnesses, let us lay aside every weight, and the sin which doth so easily beset us, and let us run with patience the race that is set before us....*" Simply put, too many Christians grow weary and quit because they're trying to carry too much weight.

What is the weight that is holding you back? What is it that keeps you in bed when you ought to be praying? What is it that keeps you at home when you ought to be sitting under the teaching of the Word? What keeps you from tithing and giving? It is sin, slothfulness and idleness. In other words, it is a lack of discipline.

According to Hebrews 12:1, we are to lay those things aside to successfully and *patiently* run the race that is set before us. In this context, the word *patience* does not mean, "to put up with." Biblical patience refers to "continuance." I've heard it defined as "consistently constant." That means consistently studying and speaking the Word. This includes not allowing yourself to be swayed by emotions or circumstances. Patience is simply being constantly, consistently the same, no matter the circumstances. We're told in James 1 that a double-minded man—one who is tossed to and fro—is unstable and should not expect to receive anything from God (vv. 7-8). Why is that? This kind of person lacks consistency.

Hebrews 12:2 gives yet another key to running the race: *"...Looking unto Jesus the author and finisher of our faith; who for the joy that was set before him endured the cross, despising the shame, and is set down at the right hand of the throne of God."* If you expect to experience the kind of victory that brings you the fullness of God's promises, you're going to have to do it by looking to Jesus.

Why do men faint? Perhaps they are focused on the wrong thing. Some have their eyes on other people, while others have their eyes on the physical manifestation of the blessings. Disciplined ones, however—the ones who make it to their due season—are the ones who are looking to Jesus. This is powerful, because He is the Author and Finisher of our faith! If you keep your eyes on Jesus, the blessings will come; if you focus too much on the blessing instead of on the Blesser, you'll grow weary and faint and will never cross the finish line.

Luke 18:1 says, *"And he [Jesus] spake a parable unto them to this end, that men ought always to pray, and not to faint."* In other words, we should pray rather than give up, cave in or quit. It always comes down to the matter of discipline.

In the coming chapters, we'll explore the relationship between discipline and the anointing and how you can cultivate both to reap an overflowing harvest of the zoé life of God.

CHAPTER THREE

Discipleship:
A Life of Discipline

As mentioned in the previous chapter, most Christians don't want to hear anything about discipline or getting their flesh under control. Many would rather focus on other topics such as prosperity, healing and deliverance. In fact, Believers will stand in line to hear the latest teaching about Bible prophecy and the Lord's return, but when you announce that you're going to talk about discipline, people don't exactly trample over each other to get a seat.

Did Jesus think discipline was important? You had better believe it! He used the root of the word *discipline* to identify those who followed Him and His example; He called them His disciples. A *disciple* is literally "a disciplined one." Read Matthew 16:24-26 to see what Jesus had to say about following Him:

> *...If any man will come after me, let him deny himself, and take up his cross, and follow me. For whosoever will save his life shall lose it: and whosoever will lose his life for my sake shall find it. For what is a man profited, if he shall gain the whole world, and lose his own soul? Or what shall a man give in exchange for his soul?*

Jesus gave us another indicator of discipleship in John 15:8: "*Herein is my Father glorified, that ye bear much fruit; so shall ye be my disciples.*" Why did Jesus say that the bearing of spiritual fruit was the test of true discipleship? It takes discipline to bear fruit. When the Lord began to deal with me on this subject, I asked myself, *Am I a disciplined person? In what areas am I disciplined? In what areas do I lack discipline? Why am I undisciplined in those areas?* Then I turned to the Word of God for answers.

Get Understanding

One of the first things I noticed was that the word *discipline* not only means, "disciplined one," it also means, "a learner," or "one who receives instruction." This is a very important point. Discipline involves learning what to embrace and what to avoid. It involves understanding God's standards and keys to successful living. It requires being open to instruction from the Holy Spirit and the Word of God.

Are you open to receiving instruction from the Word regarding self-control and discipline? If so, let's begin with an understanding of the source and nature of this battle. There is nothing more disheartening and defeating than to feel like a prisoner of your flesh. The Apostle Paul painted a picture of this battle between flesh and spirit in Romans 7:15-16: *"For that which I do I allow not: for what I would, that do I not; but what I hate, that do I. If then I do that which I would not, I consent unto the law that it is good."*

Does this sound familiar? Paul is simply saying, "I don't understand myself. I fail to do the things I want to do, and I end up doing the things that I don't want to." Who among us hasn't felt like this at one time or another? I have often heard people say, "I want to start eating healthy and exercising, but I just seem to keep falling into the same old patterns." As Jesus told His disciples when they couldn't "tarry one hour" with Him in prayer and kept falling asleep: *"...the spirit indeed is willing, but the flesh is weak"* (Matthew 26:41).

For example, let's say you begin watching an infomercial for exercise equipment. You look at the trim, toned, muscular model and say to yourself, *That could be me. I can do that!* Armed with motivation and resolve, you become a member of your neighborhood health club. Of course you have to look trendy, so you buy new workout clothes and a $100 pair of Air-something-or-other shoes. You arrive for your first workout looking good, feeling motivated and ready to sweat. In other words, you have a willing spirit. You choose a piece of high-tech, state-of-the-art exercise equipment and vow to stay on it until you've burned 400 calories or spent an hour, whichever comes first. You begin.

After what seems like a painful eternity, you look at the clock: only three minutes have elapsed. You've burned a total of 11 calories. After another three or four minutes of pain, you stop. Your willingness has been washed away in a rising tide of weak, screaming flesh.

Paul provides greater detail in Romans 7:17-24 about this struggle between the part of us that desires to please God and the part that wants nothing more than to please self:

Now then it is no more I that do it, but sin that dwelleth in me. For I know that in me (that is, in my flesh,) dwelleth no good thing: for to will is present with me; but how to perform that which is good I find not. For the good that I would I do not: but the evil which I would not, that I do. Now if I do that I would not, it is no more I that do it, but sin that dwelleth in me. I find then a law, that, when I would do good, evil is present with me. For I delight in the law of God after the inward man: But I see another law in my members, warring against the law of my mind, and bringing me into captivity to the law of sin which is in my members. O wretched man that I am! Who shall deliver me from the body of this death?

Paul is describing a war between the flesh, which he says contains no good thing, and the part of himself that delights in the law of God he calls the "inward man." This struggle between his flesh and spirit left him thinking, "O *wretched man that I am! Who shall deliver me?...!*" "*There is therefore now no condemnation to them which are in Christ Jesus, who walk not after the flesh, but after the Spirit. For the law of the Spirit of life in Christ Jesus hath made me free from the law of sin and death*" (Romans 8:1-2). To break the cycle of defeat and condemnation, we must walk after the Spirit, not after the flesh.

When you walk after the Spirit, you feed your spirit-man until it dominates your flesh. A man or a woman who does so won't be defeated for very long. All of this goes right back to the heart of what we're talking about—being disciples. There are five things God is looking for in a true disciple. In the following pages, you'll discover what they are.

CHAPTER FOUR

The Making
of a Disciple

God is not looking for mere church attendees or people who put on a good show. His eyes aren't roaming throughout the earth in search of those who talk a good talk. No, He's looking for disciples—disciplined ones who will walk after the Spirit rather than after the flesh. Being a disciple isn't easy; if it were, every Believer would be one. But the rewards of being a good disciple are great.

In studying the Word of God, I have discovered five basic requirements for being a disciple of Jesus. Think of these as characteristics exhibited by true disciplined ones. Cultivate these characteristics, and you will reap the rewards of discipleship.

1. Bear the cross.

Are you a follower of Jesus? Before answering too quickly, consider the words He spoke in Matthew 16:24: *"...If any man will come after me, let him deny himself, and take up his cross, and follow me."*

Many people have professed a desire to follow Jesus' example. They say they intend to follow Him, but, as Jesus Himself points out, the price of walking in His footsteps is high. Basically, it will cost you everything you have and are. Look at Matthew 16:24 in the *Amplified Bible*:

Then Jesus said to His disciples, If anyone desires to be My disciple, let him deny himself [disregard, lose sight of, and forget himself and his own interests] and take up his cross and follow Me [cleave steadfastly to Me, conform wholly to My example in living and, if need be, in dying, also].

This may be hard on the flesh. When you start describing discipleship in these terms, you begin losing folks in a hurry. Many will say to themselves, *Hey, I didn't sign up for that! I like that prosperity business, but nobody said anything about denying yourself and taking up a cross!*

The fact remains that to be disciplined and reap God's greater blessings, you must let go of your own interests. If you want to have everything the Bible says you have a right to, you must die to self. That's the essence of the phrase "take up your cross." You take up your cross when you take up the cause of Jesus. As we read in the *Amplified Bible*, it means to "cleave steadfastly" to Jesus and conform wholly to His example in living. It also means being prepared to die for Him if necessary, just as Jesus laid down His life for us.

2. Renounce the enemies of discipline.

We find the second requirement of discipleship in a verse that is confusing to many people and frequently misunderstood: "...*If any man come to me, and hate not his father, and mother, and wife, and children, and brethren, and sisters, yea, and his own life also, he cannot be my disciple*" (Luke 14:26).

Many people see the word "hate" in this verse and stumble over it. It's hard to imagine Jesus telling anyone to hate his or her loved ones in order to be His disciple. To properly understand this verse, you must realize that Jesus was using a figure of speech to make a point. An examination of Luke 14:26 (AMP) should shed some light on its meaning:

> ...*If anyone comes to Me and does not hate his [own] father and mother [in the sense of indifference to or relative disregard for them in comparison with his attitude toward God] and [likewise] his wife and children and brothers and sisters—[yes] and even his own life also—he cannot be My disciple.*

What Jesus is saying here is that to be a true disciple, your love for God and the things of God must be so strong that it makes your love for your family and friends look like hate in comparison. I call this the "principle of renunciation." You renounce anything that adversely affects your devotion to Jesus. In other words, to be a disciplined one, you must renounce anything that is an enemy to your discipline where the things of God are concerned.

I frequently hear family responsibilities being used as an excuse for avoiding the things of God. I have heard people say, "I'd like to pray, but I have too much to do in attending to my children." If your love for the things of God is top priority, you'll wake up before your children do to spend time with the Lord. You'll do whatever is necessary to maintain your spiritual discipline.

It really bothers me when I hear people say things like, "Well, I really wanted to come to the meeting, Brother Dollar, but my relatives were in town and they don't believe like we do. I just didn't want to cause any friction." Far too many Christians put the concerns, preferences or approval of their relatives and friends above their devotion to Christ. To be a disciplined one, you *must* renounce the enemies that attack your discipline. Compared to your love for God, your love for other people and things should look like hate.

3. Leave all.

As I told you at the beginning of this chapter, being a disciple isn't easy on your flesh. It isn't for cowards, sluggards or for the faint-hearted. The third requirement of being a disciple brings this truth home. In Luke 14:33, Jesus tells us that there is a certain kind of person who cannot be His disciple: *"So likewise, whosoever he be of you that forsaketh not all that he hath, he cannot be my disciple."*

A true disciple of Christ is one who is willing to forsake all. What Jesus is referring to here is an excessive attachment to material possessions, which is one of the most frequent barriers to Believers' becoming true disciples of Jesus. That's why it is important for people who have begun to prosper in God to never forget that He is their Source for every good thing. The Lord gave the Israelites similar advice the evening before they possessed the Promised Land (Deuteronomy 8:13-18):

And when thy herds and thy flocks multiply, and thy silver and thy gold is multiplied, and all that thou hast is multiplied; Then thine heart be lifted up, and thou forget the Lord thy God, which brought thee forth out of the land of Egypt, from the house of bondage; Who led thee through that great and terrible wilderness, wherein were fiery serpents, and scorpions, and drought, where there was no water; who brought thee forth water out of the rock of flint; Who fed thee in the wilderness with manna, which thy fathers knew not, that he might humble thee, and that he might prove thee, to do thee good at thy latter end; And thou say in thine heart, My power and the might of mine hand hath gotten me this wealth. But thou shalt remember the Lord thy God: for it is he that giveth thee power to get wealth, that he may establish his covenant which he sware unto thy fathers, as it is this day.

You must ensure that when God gives you things, you remember what He has done for you. If you maintain that "attitude of gratitude," you won't have any trouble when the Lord speaks to you concerning those things. Have the mindset that those things belong to God, not to you.

The good news is that a person who is prepared to forsake all to follow Jesus will experience increase, not decrease. One day the disciples were sitting around talking about all they had given up to follow Jesus. What was Jesus' response? Mark 10:29-30 says:

> ...Verily I say unto you, There is no man that hath left house, or brethren, or sisters, or father, or mother, or wife, or children, or lands, for my sake, and the gospel's, But he shall receive an hundredfold now in this time, houses, and brethren, and sisters, and mothers, and children, and lands, with persecutions; and in the world to come eternal life.

When God asks you to sow something, have increase on your mind. If, on the other hand, you are so attached to your material possessions that you're not prepared to forsake them, you'll never experience the God-kind of increase. Even worse, Jesus said that if you are this type of person, you cannot be His disciple.

4. Continue steadfastly.

The fourth requirement of discipleship is found in John 8:31. If you want proof of whether or not you're a true disciple, check your level of steadfastness. Jesus said to those Jews who believed in him, "...If ye continue in my word, then are ye my disciples indeed." According to Strong's Concordance, the Greek word for continue in this verse means, "to stay (in a given place, state, relation or expectancy): to abide, continue, dwell, endure, be present, remain or stand." If you remain steadfast in the Word, then you are indeed a disciplined one. What is the result of being a steadfast disciple? Jesus tells us in the very next verse: "And ye shall know the truth, and the truth shall make you free" (verse 32).

Do you need to be made free in a certain area of your life? Continuing to live steadfastly according to God's Word is the key to your breakthrough. You must be prepared to continue doing the Word, not just hearing it (James 1:22). I say this after having personally counseled people with various issues. When I shared with them a certain principle from God's Word concerning their situation, they often would say, "Oh, I tried that."

Doing something once or twice never gets anyone lasting results. Half-heartedly trying out God's principles won't do you any good either. It takes consistency and steadfastness to *know* and *apply* the truth—that is what sets you free. In fact, that's what Galatians 6:9 means when it says, *"And let us not be weary in well doing: for in due season we shall reap, if we faint not."* It's talking about the hard-nosed, bulldog, tenacious steadfastness that brings about your due season.

5. Bear the fruit of the Spirit.

John 15:8 (NASB) says, *"My Father is glorified by this, that you bear much fruit, and so prove to be My disciples."*

The ultimate test of discipleship is fruit-bearing. In John 15:9-10, Jesus talks about the fruit of the Spirit, which is love: *"As the Father hath loved me, so have I loved you: continue ye in my love. If ye keep my commandments, ye shall abide in my love; even as I have kept my Father's commandments, and abide in his love."* When you bear love and cultivate its aspects (Galatians 5:22-23)—joy, peace, patience, meekness, goodness, gentleness, faithfulness and self-control—you are proving that you are a true disciple of Jesus. This tells me that if a Christian is not walking in love, he can forget about the blessings that come with being a disciple.

You're probably very familiar with what the Apostle Paul said in 1 Corinthians 13:1-3 (AMP) about those who fail to bear the fruit of love:

If I [can] speak in the tongues of men and [even] of angels, but have not love (that reasoning, intentional, spiritual devotion such as is inspired by God's love for and in us), I am only a noisy gong or a clanging cymbal. And if I have prophetic powers (the gift of interpreting the divine will and purpose), and understand all the secret truths and mysteries and possess all knowledge, and if I have [sufficient] faith so that I can remove mountains, but have not love (God's love in me) I am nothing (a useless nobody). Even if I dole out all that I have [to the poor in providing] food, and if I surrender my body to be burned or in order that I may glory, but have not love (God's love in me), I gain nothing.

Simply put, all the religious terminology and actions in the world are a waste of time unless you're walking in the fruit of the Spirit.

*   *   *   *   *

These are the things that Jesus said would characterize those who are His disciplined ones. If you want to overcome slothfulness and reach your "expected end," make sure each is evident in your life.

CHAPTER FIVE

From Slothfulness to Diligence

Reading this chapter may be hard on your flesh. In fact, you will have to keep yourself from becoming offended and tempted to toss this book aside without finishing it. Allow me to encourage you not to dismiss what I share. I'm confident that if you will hear what the Spirit of God wants to communicate to you, not only will it be a blessing to you, but it will absolutely change your life for the better as well. God has answers to questions you may have had for years; therefore, don't allow your flesh to cause you to stumble and miss what He has for you.

Thus far, we have discussed how Satan uses slothfulness to hinder you from experiencing God's best in these last days. We have also discussed the fact that God's antidote for slothfulness is *discipline*. You may wonder how you can know if you're being slothful in an area of your life, and whether or not you have to be a full-blown, do-nothing couch potato to be slothful in the eyes of God.

It's possible to be active and diligent in one area of your life and slothful in another. For example, some people are quite disciplined where their eating is concerned, yet lack discipline when it comes to spending time in God's Word. That's why it is important to shine the light of the Word into every corner of our lives to zero in on pockets of slothfulness that keep us from experiencing God's blessings or fulfilling our destinies in Him.

The Way Out

Once you've identified the presence of slothfulness in any area of your life, the next step is to root it out. Diligence is the way out of slothfulness.

It's important that you fully explore what the Bible has to say about sloth-fulness and diligence. The book of Proverbs has a lot to say about slothful-ness. One word that Proverbs frequently uses to describe a slothful person is *sluggard*.

Proverbs 6:6-8 says, *"Go to the ant, thou sluggard; consider her ways, and be wise: Which having no guide, overseer, or ruler, provideth her meat in the summer, and gathereth her food in the harvest."* The Hebrew word in this verse that is translated *sluggard* is *atsel*. According to the *Strong's Concordance*, it literally means, "slothful." Therefore, we can accurately translate Proverbs 6:6 to read, *"Go to the ant, [you slothful one]...."* Why does the Word of God tell us to observe the ant? Ants possess a certain attribute that a slothful person needs to recognize and imitate.

There is wisdom to glean from studying the activities of ants. Whenever I have noticed ants around my house, one thing has always been true of their activity—they are always in motion. I don't believe I've ever seen ants being still, unless they are dead. That's consistency. In fact, they epitomize being "con-sistently the same," which is the true definition of patience. They consistently and methodically work toward their objective until it is achieved.

There is another truth concerning ants that we should consider in the pas-sage we just read. Verses 7-8 say, *"...Which having no guide, overseer, or ruler, provideth her meat in the summer, and gathereth her food in the harvest."* The ant does whatever it takes to bring in a harvest without having to be told, begged, supervised, threatened, overseen or prodded in any way.

If only all Believers were as diligent as ants! Imagine what the church could accomplish if all Christians had the diligence and drive to spend time with God, study His Word and stand in faith and patience without having to be constantly reminded and cajoled! We would operate in continual victory, freedom and prosperity. Furthermore, we'd be able to send the Gospel message throughout the entire world, *and* we'd be enjoying the blessings of heaven!

Do you want more insight to overcome slothfulness? Proverbs 6:9-11 says, *"How long wilt thou sleep, O sluggard? when wilt thou arise out of thy sleep? Yet a little sleep, a little slumber, a little folding of the hands to sleep: So shall thy pover-ty come as one that travelleth, and thy want as an armed man."* Notice that poverty came to this person when he chose to be idle rather than diligent. The devil didn't make him idle. Slothfulness is an act of the will, not a result of circumstances.

What you are experiencing now is a direct result of your past and present choices. If you're living in poverty, don't blame the devil, the government or another race for your "lousy luck." The Word of God makes it very clear that poverty is a result of slothfulness—end of story. Proverbs 13:4 sheds more light on the difference between slothfulness and diligence: *"The soul of the sluggard* [slothful person] *desireth, and hath nothing: but the soul of the diligent shall be made fat."* Simply put, the idle man always craves things, but he never has anything. "Oh, I wish I had a better car," the sluggard says, but he refuses to do what is necessary to obtain one.

"If only" becomes the constant excuse and complaint of the slothful person. People such as this never do anything but dream and wish. They never get the opportunity to live out their dreams, because they are not willing to do what it takes to cause those things to come to pass.

A slothful person's days are not only unproductive, according to Proverbs 15:19 (*NASB*), they are also difficult: *"The way of the lazy* [slothful] *is as a hedge of thorns, but the path of the upright is a highway."* Have you ever tried to make your way through a field of thick, waist-high briars and thorns? It's a hard, slow and painful process. That is precisely what life is like for the slothful man. For him, progress is a struggle. The sluggard goes from one bad situation to the next. It is different with the diligent, or upright, person. A diligent man finds that life's path is like an unobstructed highway. He accomplishes things and moves forward.

Proverbs has more to say about the life of the sluggard. For example, according to Proverbs 20:4, slothful people are easily discouraged by discomfort or adversity. The sluggard won't plow when it's cold; therefore, he'll have to beg during harvest time. Diligence involves being willing to have your flesh endure a little discomfort for a season. It requires a willingness to stand in the face of adversity without becoming discouraged and quitting.

Along with discomfort and discouragement, there is another tool the enemy uses with great effect in the life of a sluggard. That tool is *fear.* The slothful man says, "I can't go out and work today. I heard there was a lion on the loose. I'm just going to stay in bed!" (Proverbs 26:13).

When a person has slothful tendencies, fear can be used to keep him from doing those things that will bring him increase and blessing. I see it all the time. I see people allowing fear of rejection, fear of failure, fear of sickness, fear of harm and a host of other fears to keep them from doing the things that position them for promotion and harvest. As a result, they either literally or figuratively "stay in bed."

That's exactly what verse 14 talks about: *"As the door turneth upon its hinges, so doth the slothful upon his bed."* Therefore, the next time the alarm goes off and you're tempted to blow off your quiet time and just roll over for a little more sleep, bring this image to your remembrance—a door swinging back and forth on its hinges. The swinging door is an invitation to the devil. Slothfulness makes you vulnerable to destruction.

Worst of all, once you are highly developed in slothfulness, you won't accept correction. No one can tell you anything. According to verse 16, the biggest know-it-alls in the world are those who won't do anything: *"The sluggard is wiser in his own eyes than seven men who can give a discreet answer"* (NASB).

Your "House" and Your "Field"

In numerous places throughout Scripture, our physical bodies are referred to as tents, temples or houses (1 Corinthians 3:16; 1 Corinthians 6:19; 2 Corinthians 6:16; 2 Corinthians 5:1-4; 1 Peter 2:5).

Notice what Ecclesiastes 10:18 says about how living slothfully affects your house: *"By much slothfulness the building decayeth; and through idleness of the hands the house droppeth through."* Read this verse using the *New American Standard Bible*: *"Through indolence* [loafing, laziness, sluggishness] *the rafters sag, and through slackness the house leaks."*

I know far too many Christians whose bodies are malfunctioning because they allow slothfulness to take root in their lives. Decay is the inevitable result of being a sluggish Believer. When you start being lazy about praying, reading the Word and sitting under anointed teaching, decay will result. It grieves me to see Believers physically destroyed because of slothfulness.

Just as the Bible uses the metaphor of a house to symbolize your body, it also uses the symbol of a field to describe your life: *"For we are God's fellow workers; you are God's field, God's building"* (1 Corinthians 3:9, NASB). When you are born again, God plants some things in your life. Like a farmer, He begins working in you to produce a harvest. That is why there are so many scriptures that talk about bearing fruit.

Jesus compared the human heart to various kinds of soil (Matthew 13)—some which accept and nourish the seed of the Word well and others not as well. What kind of soil you are is up to you. What does this have to do with slothfulness? Proverbs 24:30-32 says:

> I went by the field of the slothful, and by the vineyard of the man void of understanding; And, lo, it was all grown over with thorns, and nettles had covered the face thereof, and the stone wall thereof was broken down. Then I saw, and considered it well: I looked upon it, and received instruction.

When you are slothful, the field of your life is a mess. It becomes overgrown with thorns. And according to Jesus' parable of the sower in Matthew 13, thorns represent the cares of this world, which choke the Word in your life (vv. 7, 22).

What else does Proverbs 24:30-32 tell us about the slothful man's field? It tells us that the stone wall of his life is broken down. When you allow slothfulness to take root in your life, the ultimate result is that God's protection is removed from your life. When that happens, you are fair game for the devil's attacks.

I have seen it happen. Slowly but surely, a Believer gets slothful in the things of God to the point where his regular quiet time falls by the wayside. He constantly finds excuses to miss church. The fundamental principles of faith such as confessing the Word, watching what he says, tithing and giving, and maintaining a high level of expectation are replaced by neglect. Soon, he has moved out from under the umbrella of God's protection. Trouble moves in because the walls are down; the results are worry and anxiety. As the thorns of care choke out more of the Word, the walls break down even further.

What I am describing is basically a self-reinforcing cycle of defeat; a downward spiral that ultimately leaves a Christian devastated and ineffective. Isn't that exactly what the Lord warned us about at the beginning of this book? Didn't the Spirit of God tell us that in a time of prayer, the enemy would attempt to use the weapon of slothfulness to keep God's people from enjoying the blessings and authority that are theirs in Christ Jesus? When you start being lazy about the things of God, a process of decay begins. How do you reverse that process or even keep it from starting? With the weapon of diligence.

The Solution for Slothfulness

We have clearly seen how the Bible describes slothfulness as a deadly enemy against Believers. Do you know that the Bible never presents a problem without also offering a solution?

Hebrews 6:11-12 says, "*And we desire that every one of you do show the same diligence to the full assurance of hope unto the end: That ye be not slothful, but followers of them who through faith and patience inherit the promises.*" In verse 11, the writer of Hebrews expresses his desire that we all "*show the same diligence.*" In the next verse he explains by saying, "*That ye be not slothful.*" Here, just as in the Old Testament verses we have already examined, diligence is presented as the opposite of and answer to slothfulness. Did you notice that overcoming slothfulness through diligence is tied directly to attaining the full assurance of hope and to being able to inherit the promises of God? Once again, God is trying to tell you that slothfulness is the enemy to your ability to experience God's highest and best.

Now we must ask ourselves, what is diligence? Why is diligence your assurance that you're going to inherit the promises? *Diligence* is defined as "a steady application of effort in any activity." I like that. Diligence describes a constant, consistent, steady effort to accomplish something. To inherit the promises of God, you must apply a steady effort to the study of the Word of God. You must continually root out sin from your life while steadily fellowshipping and communing with God.

Diligence in these areas is absolutely essential if you are going to witness the manifestation of your expected end. Why? Diligence is directly tied to your level of faith. "*But without faith it is impossible to please him: for he that cometh to God must believe that he is, and that he is a rewarder of them that diligently seek him*" (Hebrews 11:6).

Does this verse say that God is a rewarder of those who seek Him in any way they please? No. Does it say that He rewards those who occasionally seek Him? Of course not. We're clearly told that God rewards those who *diligently* seek Him. You might ask, "Brother Dollar, I come to church every chance I get, and I read my Bible occasionally. Won't God reward me for trying?" Not if you believe the Word of God. Don't expect to be rewarded with His blessings if there is no diligence associated with your seeking Him.

In my years in the ministry, I have discovered that, for most people, the reason they fail to receive is not that they don't do the "right" things; they simply don't do the *right* things *consistently*. They lack diligence and are without a steady application of persistent effort. Diligence will always produce rewards. For example, take two similar individuals and give them identical exercise and nutrition plans. At the end of one year, will both have experienced the same results? Probably not. Why? More than likely one will have applied those plans with greater diligence than the other. Who gets the better results? The one with the most diligence.

The same is true where spiritual things are concerned. I have seen people who, when they get around to praying, can pray heaven and earth together. Their only problem is that they never pray with any consistency. Their results suffer because of their lack of diligence. It is diligence that brings the reward, not cleverness, talent or good connections. Nothing but the willingness and discipline to apply steady, consistent effort will bring about your expected end.

In his 1932 speech to the agents of the New York Life Insurance Company, former President Calvin Coolidge said, "Nothing can take the place of persistence. Talent will not; nothing is more common than unsuccessful men with talent...Education will not; the world is full of educated derelicts. Persistence and determination are omnipotent. The slogan 'Press On' has solved and will always solve the problems of the human race."

I know Believers who have wonderful ideas and brilliant plans. Those ideas and plans, however, will never become a reality as those individuals simply lack the diligence necessary to bring them to pass. This is the difference between the mediocre person and the millionaire.

Can diligence really make you rich? Read Proverbs 10:4 and decide for yourself: *"He becometh poor that dealeth with a slack hand: but the hand of the diligent maketh rich."* I want you to notice something about this verse. The man who became poor wasn't totally inactive. It's not that he was not doing anything. What he *did* with a slack hand made the difference. In other words, his activity was sluggish, inconsistent and undisciplined.

Have you ever known anyone like that? Everything he does is done at half-speed. He never gives himself wholly to anything. Such a person is an employer's nightmare. He never puts in a solid day's work; however, you can be sure that on Friday he'll expect a full week's pay. This kind of person will never prosper in the long run. Poverty and lack will always characterize his life. The diligent person, on the other hand, can't help but experience increase. The Word of God promises it.

Proverbs 13:4 speaks of diligence as being a pathway to prosperity: *"The soul of the sluggard desireth, and hath nothing: but the soul of the diligent shall be made fat."* Notice that this passage does not say that the body of the diligent shall be made fat; it says his soul will. In this reference to prosperity and increase, "fat" symbolizes plenty and abundance.

The diligent person prospers in every aspect of life, because diligence brings increase to the spirit, soul and body. When you are disciplined enough to exert consistent, excellent effort, you will prosper mentally, emotionally and relationally. In fact, diligence can get you promoted to the highest levels of enterprise. We see this truth stated in Proverbs 22:29, which says, *"Seest thou a man diligent in his business? he shall stand before kings; he shall not stand before mean [obscure] men."*

Not only will the diligent person rub shoulders with rulers, he or she will also become a ruler. Proverbs 12:24 says, *"The hand of the diligent shall bear rule: but the slothful shall be under tribute."* God is looking for diligent men and women He can trust with responsibility, influence and authority. Second Peter 3:14 says, *"Wherefore, beloved, seeing that ye look for such things, be diligent that ye may be found of him in peace, without spot, and blameless."* I can assure you that He's not going to put slothful, undisciplined people over His resources.

Chapter Six

The Role of the Will

Several years ago, my wife and I were acquainted with a woman who had been a smoker for years. Her husband and children were constantly pleading with her to quit, but her reply was always the same: "I just can't. I've tried."

A few years later, her husband went on to be with the Lord. After a period of time, she met and fell in love with a wonderful man. Before long, she found herself hoping with all her heart that this gentleman would propose. One day he mentioned the fact that he could not marry a woman who smoked. Would you like to guess how long it took that woman to quit smoking? Not a month. Not a week. Not even a day. She quit smoking instantly! She made a quality decision to quit as an act of her will. Becoming an instantaneous non-smoker did not occur until she exercised her God-given will.

The human will is a powerful thing; even Jesus had to deal with it. In Luke 22:41-44, we see Him subjecting His will to the will of the Father:

And he was withdrawn from them about a stone's cast, and kneeled down, and prayed, saying, Father, if thou be willing, remove this cup from me: nevertheless not my will, but thine, be done. And there appeared an angel unto him from heaven, strengthening him. And being in an agony he prayed more earnestly: and his sweat was as it were great drops of blood falling down to the ground.

It's easy to forget that Jesus was God in human flesh. His flesh was subject to the same temptations as yours or mine. In the Garden of Gethsemane, Jesus' flesh took a look at what was ahead—rejection, mocking, beating, spitting, a crown of thorns, the whip, the nails, the weight of all of the sin of the world—and said, "Father, if Thou be willing, remove this cup from Me." Aren't you glad that Jesus followed up by saying, "Nevertheless, not My will but Thine be done"?

Jesus exercised His will by choosing to follow the will of His Father. There is no devil in hell that could have taken Jesus' life against His will. He had to willingly lay it down if He was to become the sacrificial payment for our sins. That's exactly what He said He was doing in John 10:17-18: *"Therefore doth my Father love me, because I lay down my life, that I might take it again. No man taketh it from me, but I lay it down of myself. I have power to lay it down, and I have power to take it again. This commandment have I received of my Father."*

At any time, Jesus could have called legions of angels to aid Him. But because He was fully man, He had to submit His will to the Father to carry out God's plan. The same is true for you and me. We must eliminate the mindset that says things such as:

"I'm a victim of my circumstances."

"I can't quit smoking. I'm addicted."

"I can't eat right."

"I can't control my temper."

"This is just the way I am."

"I can't get up early and spend time with God."

Real change begins with renewing your mind to biblical truth. Just as you began these bad habits as an exercise of your will, you can stop them by habitually practicing and applying the Word of God to your life.

"But Brother Dollar," you may be saying, "I've done that. I've used my will to try to change something about my life, and it didn't work!" I do realize it is likely that at one point in your life you had made a decision to change and fell flat on your face. We all have. What you must understand is that when you make a choice to do things God's way, a war is initiated. The devil is not going to leave you alone without a fight. The moment you set your will to break an addiction, you've started a war. The moment you make a quality decision to discipline yourself is the moment the war begins.

You may be asking, "Aren't I better off not even trying?" Absolutely not! As long as the devil has a stronghold of slothfulness in any area of your life, he can hinder you from experiencing God's best. If you want to see your expected end, you must be diligent. There's no way to do that without picking a fight with the devil.

Many Christians just want to stand in a prayer line, have someone lay hands on them, and "ZAP!" No more problem—instant discipline. Sorry to say, it rarely works that way. God will occasionally do a remarkable work of deliverance in someone's life; however, that is the exception, not the rule.

The War Against Your Soul

You must wage a war to move from slothfulness to diligence. It's not optional. The Apostle Peter makes mention of this war in 1 Peter 2:11: *"Dearly beloved, I beseech you as strangers and pilgrims, abstain from fleshly lusts, which war against the soul."*

When most people see the word "lust," they immediately think in terms of sexual desire. That certainly is one type of lust, but it's far from being the only one. The word *lust* is defined as "a strong appetite." There are many different things after which a person can lust. Some lust after money, power or influence. Others lust for food, comfort and leisure.

An excessive appetite for anything can become lust. What did Peter say about these lusts? They war against your soul. Out-of-control appetites do more than just bring war to your mind and will. They also try to draw you away from God. James 1:13-15 says, *"Let no man say when he is tempted, I am tempted of God: for God cannot be tempted with evil, neither tempteth he any man: But every man is tempted, when he is drawn away of his own lust, and enticed. Then when lust hath conceived, it bringeth forth sin: and sin, when it is finished, bringeth forth death."*

Lust will draw you away from the things of God and push you toward those things that ultimately result in death. As in any war, the price of losing this battle is high. As James points out, it can cost you your life.

Winning the War

As in any war, the side that is strongest and most tactful wins. Concerning your life, the side of you that is stronger—your flesh or your spirit—is determined by which one is the most well nourished. Every day you do things that either feed your flesh or feed your spirit.

A desire for something grows strong only as you give attention to it. You don't suddenly "have" a strongly developed sexual appetite like you would "have" the flu. It begins when you give your attention to something like pornography or even risqué television shows. The more you expose your mind and heart to ungodly things, the stronger the desire for them grows. The more you feed it, the bigger and stronger it gets.

This trap is deadly, because while you're feeding a fleshy desire, you are almost certainly neglecting to feed your spirit. If you're focusing on pornography, you are not going to be spending time with God. It's no wonder that, when you finally try to use your will to change your behavior, you fail! You have a strong, highly developed desire and a puny, undernourished, underdeveloped spirit.

So how do you reverse that condition? First, cut off nourishment to the ungodly desire. Second, do the things that bring the power of God on the scene, chiefly by using your faith. In fact, anything you seek to accomplish as a Believer must be done by faith. Believing God for the strength to break an addiction is no different than believing Him for a new bicycle. Find a scripture on which to stand and meditate on it. Speak that Word and avoid saying anything contrary to it.

Third, add corresponding action to your faith. James 2:20 tells us that faith without corresponding action is dead. That's why it is so important to begin this process by cutting off the flow of nourishment to the desire that you are trying to overcome. If diligence is ever going to replace slothfulness in your life, your spirit and its desires must be stronger than the cravings of your flesh.

CHAPTER SEVEN

A Disciplined Mind

So far in our study, we have explored the need to gain control of the flesh and what it takes to do so. However, the fact is that if you are going to discipline yourself to pray, eat healthy or to abstain from destructive and addictive things, you must address your thought life. Thoughts are not harmless, innocent, meaningless flashes in the circuitry of your brain. According to the Word of God, thoughts have consequences. Thoughts have power and lead to actions, and those actions turn into habits.

Before we delve more deeply into understanding the power of disciplining your thoughts, I want you to take a look at Hebrews 12:1-3:

Wherefore seeing we also are compassed about with so great a cloud of witnesses, let us lay aside every weight, and the sin which doth so easily beset us, and let us run with patience the race that is set before us, looking unto Jesus the author and finisher of our faith; who for the joy that was set before him endured the cross, despising the shame, and is set down at the right hand of the throne of God. For consider him that endured such contradiction of sinners against himself, lest ye be wearied and faint in your minds.

The first thing we learn from this passage is that if we are going to make it all the way to the end of the race, we must lay some things aside. What things? Weight and sin. You can't successfully run the race of life while carrying around heavy weights, such as negative habits, undisciplined flesh and sin. As I have reiterated throughout this book, if you're going to experience all that God has for you, you must become disciplined—and that means losing "dead weight."

Notice in Hebrews 12:3 that the writer says, *"For consider him [Jesus] that endured such contradiction of sinners against himself, lest ye be wearied and faint in your minds.*" God's Word instructs us to do something here. We are told to "consider" Jesus. Considering is done in your mind. We are not being told to consider Jesus simply to give us something to do. The Word says to do it, because there is a benefit in it. What is the benefit? Not getting weary in your mind and fainting. In the long history of the Olympic games, no one ever won a race who fainted on the third lap. You can't win if you faint. Likewise, according to this scripture, you're in danger of fainting if you are mentally weary.

As we have previously seen, the mind is part of man's soulish realm. The mind, will and emotions comprise the soul. In addition, there are two other realms—the spirit and body. You are a spirit who possesses a soul, and you live in a physical body. Therefore, if you don't consider the Word (Jesus, the Word made flesh according to John 1:14), you will become weary and will mentally faint.

It's important to understand that the mind is the arena of faith. It is the battleground on which you will either win or lose the fight of faith. In fact, I can't overstate how important your thought life is where faith is concerned. This is true for many reasons, including the fact that your mind is where belief takes place.

I challenge you to do a study on the words "believe" and "belief." What you will learn will enlighten you. Here are just a couple of examples:

Mark 11:23-24

For verily I say unto you, That whosoever shall say unto this mountain, Be thou removed, and be thou cast into the sea; and shall not doubt in his heart, but shall believe that those things which he saith shall come to pass; he shall have whatsoever he saith. Therefore I say unto you, What things soever ye desire, when ye pray, believe that ye receive them, and ye shall have them.

What you receive in life is directly tied to what you believe. In fact, your very salvation is a product of belief.

Romans 10:9-11

That if thou shalt confess with thy mouth the Lord Jesus, and shalt believe in thine heart that God hath raised him from the dead, thou shalt be saved. For with the heart man believeth unto righteousness; and with the mouth confession is made unto salvation. For the scripture saith, Whosoever believeth on him shall not be ashamed.

Just as belief in the truth will bring salvation and blessings, according to 2 Thessalonians 2:11-12, belief in the enemy's lies and those of this world's system will lead to curses and death: *"And for this cause God shall send them strong delusion, that they should believe a lie: That they all might be damned who believed not the truth, but had pleasure in unrighteousness."*

Belief is a product of your thought life. Your believing the truth or believing lies determines how successfully you fight on the battleground of your mind. The first step in winning this fight is acknowledging that it exists. You must face the fact that Satan is after the control of your mind, and ultimately, your behavior and life. He wants to sit in its cockpit and coerce you into cooperating with him.

The direction the pilot (your mind) sets will be the direction in which the plane (your body and actions) will go. Either the Spirit of Truth (the Holy Spirit) is in the cockpit of your mind with you, or the enemy is.

Look at what Jesus said about the role of the Holy Spirit in this regard: *"Howbeit when he, the Spirit of truth, is come, he will guide you into all the truth: for he shall not speak of himself; but whatsoever he shall hear, that shall he speak: and he will shew you things to come"* (John 16:13).

The course of your life and the nature of your actions are going to be governed by your thoughts. That is why the enemy works hard to gain access to that area. It is crucial to learn how Satan operates so he can be defeated. What is his primary plan of attack? To deceive you; to influence you into thinking the way the world thinks. That is why, in Colossians 2:8 (*NASB*), Paul says, *"See to it that no one takes you captive through philosophy and empty deception, according to the tradition of men, according to the elementary principles of the world, rather than according to Christ."*

Deception is nothing more than wrong belief. It is a belief in something that is false. What makes deception so dangerous is that at the heart of every lie there is a little kernel of truth. For example, in the Garden of Eden, Satan told Eve what God had said; he, however, left out a little and added a little. Although there was a core of truth in what he said to Eve, it was twisted. Because of Eve's deception and Adam's disobedience to God, sin entered the world. Deception will keep you from fulfilling your destiny.

Are you beginning to see how important it is to discipline your mind? It's actually the key to disciplining your flesh. Romans 12:2 clearly says so: *"And be not conformed to this world: but be ye transformed by the renewing of your mind...."* According to this verse, changing your pattern of thinking to bring it into alignment with the truth of God's Word will actually transform you. Once again, we see why deception and wrong thinking is so dangerous. It, too, can transform you—negatively.

If you're looking at yourself today and don't like what you see, you need to face the fact that who you are is a product of how you've been thinking and what you've been believing.

Satan's Messengers

When it comes to waging war in the battleground of the mind, it's important to know against whom you're fighting. In actuality, you're not just fighting your own carnal nature. You must also contend with spirit beings who try to come against your soul—the realm of your mind.

These demonic forces don't have much power or authority. They rely on your giving them access to your thought life. It's really all they have the ability to do. That is why their most frequently used weapon is the weapon of suggestion. Demonic spirits will try to suggest things to you to deceive you and to introduce false ways of thinking into your mind. Therefore, don't get the Hollywood idea that you need to worry about demons creeping around in your attic. If they are around, they're trying to creep into your thought life.

One of the most familiar passages of Scripture that describes this battle is 2 Corinthians 10:3-5:

> *For though we walk in the flesh, we do not war after the flesh: (For the weapons of our warfare are not carnal, but mighty through God to the pulling down of strong holds;) Casting down imaginations, and every high thing that exalteth itself against the knowledge of God, and bringing into captivity every thought to the obedience of Christ.*

Here the Word clearly tells us that although it may *seem* like the battleground lies in your flesh, it's really in your mind. You only see the results in your flesh.

So how is this battle fought and won? You obtain victory by *"casting down imaginations and every high thing that exalts itself against the knowledge of God and by bringing into captivity every thought to the obedience of Christ."* Imaginations and thoughts that are contrary to the Word and will of God are the seeds that, if left to grow, will ultimately become strongholds of wrong behavior and action.

Because of the nature of the battle, it is essential that you learn to do what the Bible refers to as "walking in the Spirit." Paul instructed the Galatians to

"...*Walk in the Spirit, and ye shall not fulfil the lust of the flesh*" (Galatians 5:16). Here we have a key to controlling your flesh. As we saw in a previous chapter, Paul went on to elaborate on the battle between the desires of the born-again spirit and the desires of the carnal flesh (vv. 17-18): "*For the flesh lusteth against the Spirit, and the Spirit against the flesh: and these are contrary the one to the other: so that ye cannot do the things that ye would. But if ye be led of the Spirit, ye are not under the law.*"

To get your flesh under submission, learn to walk in the Spirit. What does it mean to walk in the Spirit? It means walking according to the Word. Jesus said, "The words that I speak, are spirit and, life" (John 6:63).

When you walk in the Spirit, you feed and nourish your spirit by meditating on God's Word and spending time communing with Him. It means that you hear the voice of the Holy Spirit louder and more clearly than you hear the voice of your flesh or the voices of demonic suggestion. Walking in the Spirit also means that when you hear the voice of the Holy Spirit, you immediately obey.

Now, let me tell you what walking in the Spirit is *not*. It is not walking in presumption or religious foolishness. It also not walking around like some deep, mystical, Christian guru. I have met people who tend to over-spiritualize everything and think they're walking in the Spirit. The true "Spirit walk" is a practical one.

Of course, before you can let your Spirit walk keep you from fulfilling the lusts of the flesh, it helps to have a realistic assessment of what your flesh is capable of doing. That's what Paul gives us in Galatians 5:19-21:

> Now the works of the flesh are manifest, which are these; Adultery, fornication, uncleanness, lasciviousness, idolatry, witchcraft, hatred, variance, emulations, wrath, strife, seditions, heresies, envyings, murders, drunkenness, revellings, and such like: of the which I tell you before, as I have also told you in time past, that they which do such things shall not inherit the kingdom of God.

I want you to notice something here. Verse 19 did not refer to these horrible things as works of the devil. Instead, Paul called them works of the flesh. Isn't that interesting? We shouldn't blame the devil for the wickedness in our lives. According to the Word of God, it's a product of our flesh when it is given its own way. You must take responsibility for the darkness in your life. The only role the devil plays is getting us to entertain ungodly thoughts. Deception leaves your flesh free to produce works like those listed above.

In the middle of that list is a word we don't hear very often these days—*lasciviousness*. It's a word few Christians understand. In the next chapter, we're going to examine its meaning.

CHAPTER EIGHT

Lasciviousness

Webster's Dictionary defines *lasciviousness* as "a tendency to be unrestrained." A life of lasciviousness is a way of living in which there is little or no control over the appetites of the flesh. If you eat whatever you feel like eating, eat as much of it as you want and don't exercise restraint, you're lascivious in that area. If you don't climb out of bed until you're good and ready, you're lascivious where sleep is concerned. If you gratify your sexual cravings any way you please, that too is lasciviousness. In fact, it's possible to be lascivious in almost any area in which your flesh has an appetite or a need.

In the previous chapter, we saw that lasciviousness was listed among the works of the flesh (Galatians 5:19-21), along with fornication, witchcraft and murder. Make no mistake—having unrestrained flesh is serious business in the eyes of God, because it keeps you from fulfilling His plan for your life. The inability to control your eating habits will derail your calling just as surely as adultery will.

If I seem to be talking a lot about food and eating in this book, it's for a good reason. I'm convinced that lasciviousness regarding food is the cause of more spiritual shipwrecks and human failures than almost any other appetite. It's no accident that Eve's temptation in the Garden of Eden involved food (Genesis 3:1). You'll also remember that Satan's first temptation of Jesus in the wilderness was food-related (Luke 4:3).

Obviously, the enemy knows something about lasciviousness. If food was the initial point of attack against the First Adam and the Last Adam (Jesus), then perhaps we should make sure that we're not being deceived in this area as well.

I am using the unrestrained desire for food as a frequent illustration, because it is something with which I have had personal experience. There was a time in my ministry when it became apparent that if I didn't get control of this area of my life, I would never accomplish all that the Lord had called me to do. I have always enjoyed food. For example, I used to become irritated with my wife, Taffi, when we would buy a big bag of oatmeal-raisin cookies. Why? She would reach in, pinch off a little part of a cookie and put the rest away. Me? I'd eat the whole bag in no time. Taffi was exercising restraint, while I was demonstrating lasciviousness.

The Lord spoke to me one day and said, "*If the devil can whip you over food, he can whip you over anything.*" I knew that if God was ever going to work His great power through me—if I was ever going to see the dead raised in my ministry, for example—I would have to gain control of my flesh where eating was concerned. That's why the principles I'm outlining in this book aren't just abstract theories to me. I've lived them. I know they work because they're in the Word. I'm also writing as a witness to you that I've applied those principles and have seen them work for me. This isn't theology; it's life.

There are some things you are uniquely called to do. Satan knows it, and he's going to do his best to keep you from fulfilling that high calling. The most effective way for him to do that is to get you into lasciviousness in some area of your life.

The Mind and Lasciviousness

In the previous chapter, we saw that the mind is a battleground, and what happens there determines what you do in the flesh. As you would expect, this is also true where lasciviousness is concerned. How does your thought life result in lasciviousness? The Word clearly shows us in Ephesians 4:17-20:

> *This I say therefore, and testify in the Lord, that ye henceforth walk not as other Gentiles walk, in the vanity of their mind, having the understanding darkened, being alienated from the life of God through the ignorance that is in them, because of the blindness of their heart: Who being past feeling have given themselves over unto lasciviousness, to work all uncleanness with greediness. But ye have not so learned Christ.*

This passage of Scripture shows us the progression of lasciviousness—how it begins with a vain mind and a darkened understanding. A darkened mind leads to giving oneself over to lasciviousness to work all uncleanness with greediness.

Pay close attention to the wording of the last verse. Notice that it says these people had "*given* themselves over" to lasciviousness. Lasciviousness doesn't just jump on you and take control of your body. It progressively and gradually becomes the norm in your life as you give yourself over to it. In other words, it is a result of your choices. You don't just wake up one morning after years of being disciplined and suddenly abandon all restraint in some area of your life. Inch by inch, step by step, you remove the restraints until one day you find your flesh calling the shots.

It's like the old story of the frog in the kettle. This all-purpose, instructive anecdote states that if you put a frog in a pan of hot water, he'll jump out because he's uncomfortable. But if you put that frog in a kettle of cool water and then gradually turn up the heat under it, the frog will eventually boil to death without ever jumping out. The frog gets accustomed to each rise in temperature and doesn't realize he's in a deadly situation until it's too late.

The same is true for many Believers concerning the restraints on their flesh. They gradually cast off restraints a little at a time. They don't realize how dominant their flesh has become until the deadly force of lasciviousness is threatening to destroy them spiritually and physically. It begins as a tiny seed that, unless uprooted, will ultimately become a massive tree. The seed of lasciviousness is a thought, and its end result is an unrestrained life that is headed for destruction.

There are basically three areas in which lasciviousness can be present in your life:

- Lasciviousness of the mind (thoughts).
- Lasciviousness of the mouth (words).
- Lasciviousness of the body (actions).

These three realms also represent a progression, or sequence. Unrestrained thinking ultimately leads to unrestrained talking, and unrestrained talking always results in unrestrained behavior.

To align your life with God, you must overcome lasciviousness. Are you ready to do that? If so, say these confessions aloud as a declaration of faith.

I refuse to live a lascivious life.

I will not allow my thought life to go unrestrained.

I take every thought captive to the obedience of the Anointed One and His Anointing.

I walk in the Spirit; therefore, I do not fulfill the lusts of the flesh.

I am spiritual; therefore, I think the Word, speak the Word and do the Word.

CHAPTER NINE

Pulling Down Strongholds

Have you ever had dandelion weeds in your yard? If so, you know it's not easy to get rid of them. If you simply cut one off at ground level, it will grow back bigger and stronger than before. To get rid of a dandelion, you must pull it out by the roots.

The kinds of slothful and undisciplined behavior we have discussed are like those dandelion weeds. Many people will try to get rid of them by working above the surface. They'll buy self-help books, get counseling, obtain prescriptions from their doctors or make New Year's resolutions and turn over a thousand "new leaves." All of these efforts to change are like cutting that dandelion off at ground level; they're external. It may *seem* to do some good for a time, but before long the problem comes back worse than ever.

If you want to experience true change, you must go after the root of slothful and lascivious patterns of action. The good news is that God's Word tells us how to do it. Let's start by revisiting 2 Corinthians 10:3-5:

> *For though we walk in the flesh, we do not war after the flesh: (For the weapons of our warfare are not carnal, but mighty through God to the pulling down of strong holds;) Casting down imaginations, and every high thing that exalteth itself against the knowledge of God, and bringing into captivity every thought to the obedience of Christ.*

The first thing I want you to observe about this passage is the nature and location of the battle. We're told that though we walk in a fleshy body, this battle is not a battle of the flesh. This is where most people make their first mistake. They think that if their flesh is out of control, the problem must be in their flesh. As a result, they attack the problem with carnal or natural weapons.

What kind of weapons should we use? Verse four tells us: *"(For the weapons of our warfare are not carnal, but mighty through God to the pulling down of strong holds)."* The weapons that will win your war against addictions and negative behaviors are not carnal or natural. Instead, they are mighty through God.

Think about it. What type of spiritual weapon has God placed in the hand of every Believer? The sword of the Spirit—the anointed Word of God. To win this fight, you must be heavily armed with God's Word. You have to know it, meditate on it, speak it and do it. What is this weapon good for, according to verse four? The pulling down of strongholds.

A *stronghold* is nothing more than "a demonically inspired and instigated pattern of thinking." It is a pattern that is deeply entrenched. In fact, it is just what its name suggests—a demonic hold on your thinking. Again, the battleground is in your mind, and the only effective weapon is the Word.

Not only does this passage of Scripture give us the weapon, it also gives us the strategy. In a war, it's not enough to have the most powerful weapon. You must also have the proper tactics and strategy if you want to completely defeat your enemy. We find the winning strategy in verse five: *"Casting down imaginations, and every high thing that exalteth itself against the knowledge of God, and bringing into captivity every thought to the obedience of Christ."*

Here we have another confirmation that the battleground is in your mind. The key words in this verse are *imaginations, knowledge* and *thought.* All three are in the realm of your mind, aren't they? This verse also shows us *why* God's Word is such a powerful weapon against these strongholds. You can't know whether or not something is exalting itself against the knowledge of God unless you have knowledge of God from His Word. You can't bring thoughts into captivity to the obedience of the Anointed One and His Anointing unless you know what to obey.

In this powerful passage, we are given three important keys:
- The battleground (the mind).
- The weapon (the Word).
- The strategy (casting down imaginations and taking thoughts captive).

Cleaning Your "House"

Now let's take a closer look at the demonic powers behind these strongholds. The Bible uses a "house" as a metaphor for the human body. In Matthew 12:43-45,

Jesus used this symbol to teach us some things about how demonic powers relate to human vessels:

> When the unclean spirit is gone out of a man, he walketh through dry places, seeking rest, and findeth none. Then he saith, I will return into my house from whence I came out; and when he is come, he findeth it empty, swept, and garnished. Then goeth he, and taketh with himself seven other spirits more wicked than himself, and they enter in and dwell there: and the last state of that man is worse than the first. Even so shall it be also unto this wicked generation.

First, notice that Jesus said, "When the unclean spirit is gone out of a man...." This tells us that some spirits are unclean. There are spiritual beings, called demons, who are vile, filthy and perverse. It also tells us that they can inhabit a human body; otherwise, they couldn't "go out" of a man.

The second thing I want you to notice is that these spirits seek a place to rest. They need a place to dwell. When Jesus cast a legion of demons out of the madman of Gadara, they begged to be sent into a herd of pigs (Matthew 8:28-32). Before I go any further, I want to clarify something. There is a lot of bad theology and strange thinking in the church where demons are concerned.

People these days generally tend to take one of two stances. The first is that they don't believe demons are real. They think the Bible only talks about them because people back in those days didn't have the medical knowledge we do today. The second is that they see demons under every rock and behind every tree. They think every symptom, craving, tendency and twitch is a devil. Some sincere Christians are actually terrified that they'll become demonically possessed. The Bible truth actually lies between those two extremes.

Demons are real. Jesus Himself says so on several occasions in Scripture. The Bible teaches that they are fallen angels who joined Lucifer in his rebellion against God and were cast out of heaven (Isaiah 14:12-17; Daniel 8:10-11; Luke 10:18; Revelation 12:4).

A demon can possess an unbeliever, but a demon cannot dwell in a genuinely born-again Christian. Let me repeat that for emphasis: A demon cannot dwell in a Christian. How do I know that? Because the Bible teaches that when you are born again, Jesus comes to live within you. Colossians 1:27 says, "...Christ in you, the hope of glory...." If you're saved, Jesus is inside of you—and I can assure you that He's not about to share a house with the devil!

The final thing I want you to see from the parable Jesus told about the house is that when the demons were driven out, it was cleaned up but left empty: *"Then [the demon] says, 'I will return to my house from which I came'; and when it comes, it finds it unoccupied, swept, and put in order"* (Matthew 12:44, NASB). Many unbelievers manage to clean up the house of their lives for a time; however, their solution is only a temporary fix. Unless they fill it with Jesus, they'll be worse off than before they started.

If you've never made Jesus the Lord of your life, there will never be a better time than right now. Invite Him into your heart and surrender control of your future to Him. You don't want to do a temporary clean-up and then leave your "house" empty. Second Peter 2:20-21 says:

> For if after they have escaped the pollutions of the world through the knowledge of the Lord and Saviour Jesus Christ, they are again entangled therein, and overcome, the latter end is worse with them than the beginning. For it had been better for them not to have known the way of righteousness, than, after they have known it, to turn from the holy commandment delivered unto them.

Bind the "Strong Man"

Jesus' parable of the cleansed house was not the only illustration He used to explain how the enemy attempts to take up residence in someone's life. We find another instance in Luke 11:17-20. The Pharisees had accused Jesus of casting out demons through the power of Beelzebub—the captain of the demons. Jesus responded by saying:

> ...Every kingdom divided against itself is brought to desolation; and a house divided against a house falleth. If Satan also be divided against himself, how shall his kingdom stand? Because ye say that I cast out devils through Beelzebub. And if I by Beelzebub cast out devils, by whom do your sons cast them out? Therefore shall they be your judges. But if I with the finger of God cast out devils, no doubt the kingdom of God is come upon you.

Once Jesus had answered the Pharisees' accusation, He proceeded to use the opportunity to do some teaching about how Satan takes up residence in a man's life and how the power of the Anointed One can set the same man free. Verses 21-22 say, *"When a strong man armed keepeth his palace, his goods are in peace: But when a stronger than he shall come upon him, and overcome him, he taketh from him all his armour wherein he trusted, and divideth his spoils."*

Here is what I want you to see. When a stronghold (the strong man) is deeply entrenched in a person's thinking, natural means will not be enough to move him out. However, when someone stronger and more anointed—Jesus, the incarnate Word of God—shows up, that stronghold is broken, overpowered and kicked out!

Here is how this works for us today. The armor that protects a demonic stronghold is an ungodly pattern of thinking and an unholy attitude. An unbiblical thought life represents the stronghold's walls of containment. Remember, Jesus and the Word are the same. He was the Word made flesh. Therefore, when you begin to replace unbiblical thoughts with thoughts from the Word, you are bringing the Stronger One into your house to bind the strong man. When you begin to take thoughts captive to the obedience of the Anointed One and His Anointing, it's like bringing Jesus Himself into your mind to overpower the enemy and plunder his goods.

The continued presence of a stronghold in your life depends on your continuing to have thoughts, opinions and attitudes that are not aligned with God's Word. As soon as you begin to bring them into alignment, that stronghold undergoes heavy attack. The more areas you align with God's truth, the fewer strongholds you will have in your mind.

It would be nice if the moment we were born again all our thinking and attitudes automatically switched over to truth. Regrettably, it doesn't work that way. Yes, your spirit is instantly reborn, but your mind must be completely renewed. That's why Paul said in Romans 12:2, "And be not conformed to this world: but be ye transformed by the renewing of your mind, that ye may prove what is that good, and acceptable, and perfect, will of God."

Becoming born again is not the conclusion of the process of salvation; it is only the beginning. Once you are saved, you must go to work, replacing all of your old ways of thinking with God's ideas, attitudes and viewpoints. It is only then that strongholds will be pulled down and you'll see lasting changes in your behavior.

Adults spend 30, 40, 50 years and longer having their ideas shaped by the world. They allow parents, friends and the media to shape their thinking, then they expect to change their life in one revival service. It simply doesn't work that way. That is why we must recall the characteristic of *persistence* that we discussed earlier in this book. Persistence is your willingness to "stick with it" until it's done. Will you encounter resistance as you begin this process? Certainly! The devil will throw all kinds of things your way to distract you from getting into the Word and praying regularly.

Make a quality decision to study the Bible regularly, and brace yourself for intense warfare against your mind and body. For example, be ready to get sleepy, hungry or be distracted right about the time you sit down to read your Bible. Satan knows that if the Word is firmly planted in your heart, he's a "goner!" He will no longer be able to have his way in your life. That is why persistence and consistency are so important to this process of binding the strong man.

Common Strongholds

So far, we have spoken in generalities where strongholds are concerned. Now it's time to get specific. It is rare to find a Christian who doesn't deal with at least one of the following strongholds:

Unbelief — Difficulty or inability to believe that biblical principles work and that God's promises come to pass.

Cold Love — The inability to walk in love toward others.

Fear — Consistent and often irrational fear or dread of certain things.

Unforgiveness — The inability to let go of hurts, grudges or offenses.

Lust — Appetites that are out of control, or consistent desires that are contrary to God's Word.

There are many other potential areas in which strongholds can be constructed in your mind; however, the areas I have mentioned are the most common.

In addition to all of the scriptures that we have discussed that support the principle concerning the mind and its effect on your lifestyle, there is one more that brings this truth home. Proverbs 23:7 says, "...*For as he thinketh in his heart, so is he....*" The major key to moving from slothfulness to diligence—from lasciviousness to discipline—is rooting out strongholds in your thinking.

CHAPTER TEN

Sources of Strongholds

You obviously want more discipline in your life. If that weren't true, you wouldn't be reading this book. And you certainly wouldn't have stayed with me this far if you weren't hungry to change the way you're living.

So far, we have seen that the outward behaviors we exhibit are the direct result of how we think. We've also seen that an ingrained pattern of wrong, or negative, thinking is called a stronghold. In the previous chapter, we identified what strongholds are and discovered both the weapon and the strategy for eliminating them from our lives. We also saw that strongholds are basically demonically induced patterns of thinking that are contrary to the truth of God's Word. The more deeply entrenched the thinking pattern, the more fortified the stronghold. To remove a stronghold, you must identify where it exists—in the mind.

Now that you know how to be free, I want to show you how to stay free. To do that, it's important that you understand the point of origin of strongholds. Since we know that a stronghold is constructed of wrong thoughts, ideas and attitudes, it makes sense to ask the question, "From where do these false concepts come?" If we can identify the source of these things, we are way ahead in being able to keep them from taking root in our thinking.

There are basically three tools that the enemy can use to produce strongholds in your life. In this chapter, we'll explore each one.

The World

When the New Testament refers to the "world," it's usually not referring to planet Earth. Instead, it's talking about the world system. Jesus made frequent reference to the world in this sense, such as when He said to His disciples, *"If the world hate you, ye know that it hated me before it hated you. If ye were of the world, the world would love his own: but because ye are not of the world, but I have chosen you out of the world, therefore the world hateth you"* (John 15:18-19).

The *world* is "the satanically inspired system of thinking and those who participate in it." As Jesus said in verses 18-19, this system hates God and anyone connected to Him. Basically, He said the same thing in John 17:14 as He was praying to the Father about the church: *"I have given them thy word; and the world hath hated them, because they are not of the world, even as I am not of the world."*

The world system has a ruler. Jesus spoke of this ruler just before He was betrayed: *"Hereafter I will not talk much with you: for the prince of this world cometh, and hath nothing in me"* (John 14:30). Jesus called Satan *"the prince of this world."* In saying so, He meant Satan is the ruler of the twisted, perverted part of creation that has not yet experienced redemption.

Paul made a similar reference in one of his letters to the Corinthians. Second Corinthians 4:4 says, *"...In whom the god of this world hath blinded the minds of them which believe not, lest the light of the glorious gospel of Christ, who is the image of God, should shine unto them."* Notice what Paul says about what Satan has done to those in the world system—he has blinded the minds of people. Here we clearly see that the world has a problem with its thinking. The people who operate according to the world system have had their minds blinded by the devil.

In many other places, the Word of God talks about the "wisdom of the world" or "man's wisdom." For example, in 1 Corinthians 2:4-5, Paul made it clear that he exhibited caution in not utilizing this type of fallen thinking in his presentation of the Gospel: *"And my speech and my preaching was not with enticing words of man's wisdom, but in demonstration of the Spirit and of power: That your faith should not stand in the wisdom of men, but in the power of God."*

Do you see it? The world system has ways of thinking that are wrong. It has a type of wisdom, which is corrupted. Because the world is ruled by Satan and thoroughly corrupted, all thoughts, ideas and attitudes that come out of it are perverse and false.

It is dangerous to adopt worldly attitudes and thoughts. Such corrupted thinking can produce a stronghold. That is why Apostles Paul, John, Peter and James were so forceful when talking about this subject. Take Colossians 2:8, for example: *"Beware lest any man spoil you through philosophy and vain deceit, after the tradition of men, after the rudiments of the world, and not after Christ."*

James was sterner in his warnings to Believers about becoming too cozy with the world's way of thinking. He said, *"Ye adulterers and adulteresses, know ye not that the friendship of the world is enmity with God? Whosoever therefore will be a friend of the world is the enemy of God"* (James 4:4). Now that's laying it on the line, isn't it? You can't adopt the world's viewpoint on matters and remain a friend of God. The world hates God—Jesus said so. Here is what John had to say on the subject (1 John 2:15-17):

> *Love not the world, neither the things that are in the world. If any man love the world, the love of the Father is not in him. For all that is in the world, the lust of the flesh, and the lust of the eyes, and the pride of life, is not of the Father, but is of the world. And the world passeth away, and the lust thereof: but he that doeth the will of God abideth for ever.*

In this powerful passage, he gives a quick breakdown of what you will experience when you allow worldly thoughts and attitudes to infect your thinking:

- The lust of the flesh
- The lust of the eyes
- The pride of life

This list covers the kinds of strongholds and behaviors that we're learning to overcome. Is an unhealthy appetite for food the problem? Then lust of the flesh is the source. Is inappropriate sexual desire your challenge? Then lust of the eyes is really the issue. Is a strong need for status and power your stronghold? Then the pride of life is at the root.

You can't absorb the world's thinking without getting the world's results, and those results are bondage and death! Ironically, I see Believers doing it every day. They allow family, friends, the media and a host of other sources to communicate wrong ways of thinking. Instead of comparing those deceptive thoughts to the standard of God's Word and rejecting them if they fail to measure up, many Believers simply accept them.

Let me give you an example. According to the world system, there is absolutely nothing wrong with a man and a woman being sexually active outside of marriage. Television, movies, books, magazines and the public education system often portray premarital sex as "normal." If you are acquainted with the Word of God, you know God's standard on that issue. His attitude is, "One man, one woman for life—period!" Why does God say that? He knows there is death and destruction outside of His system. He's not trying to spoil people's fun; He's trying to save their lives.

I often come across Christians who are letting the world's thinking about sex pollute their minds. They saturate their minds with messages from the popular culture and then wonder, *Does God really expect me to abstain until I'm married? He can't really mean that.* Do you see how it's possible for a worldly thought or attitude to become a stronghold? This kind of deception is particularly deadly because it is an anti-anointing. Second John 1:7 says, *"For many deceivers are entered into the world, who confess not that Jesus Christ is come in the flesh. This is a deceiver and an antichrist."*

Deception will rob you of the anointing. Without the anointing, you can't have your burdens removed and your yokes destroyed. When you allow yourself to be seduced by the world's way of thinking about things, you're actually allowing yourself to de deceived. In 1 Corinthians 3:18-20, Paul warns us about self-deception and adopting the corrupted wisdom of the world:

Let no man deceive himself. If any man among you seemeth to be wise in this world, let him become a fool, that he may be wise. For the wisdom of this world is foolishness with God. For it is written, He taketh the wise in their own craftiness. And again, The Lord knoweth the thoughts of the wise, that they are vain.

In a similar vein, James warns us about allowing ourselves to buy into the world's wisdom (James 3:15-17):

This wisdom descendeth not from above, but is earthly, sensual, devilish. For where envying and strife is, there is confusion and every evil work. But the wisdom that is from above is first pure, then peaceable, gentle, and easy to be intreated, full of mercy and good fruits, without partiality, and without hypocrisy.

The world system is sending you a steady stream of thoughts, ideas and attitudes. If you take every thought captive to the obedience of Christ and cast down every high thing that exalts itself above the knowledge of God, you're not going to be infected by them. If, on the other hand, you allow the world to color your thinking, you're susceptible to the construction of a stronghold, and I can assure you that you won't like the end result.

Your Personal Experiences and Conclusions

The world system isn't the only source of potential strongholds. There is another avenue I see being used against Believers all the time. The avenue is within them.

We all have a tendency to view the world through the lens of our own experience. Our perception of reality is greatly influenced by our past experiences and the conclusions we draw from them. There is, however, a problem with that. Your experience is not necessarily a valid standard of truth. Your finite, human mind doesn't always draw valid conclusions. The only infallible, accurate standard for truth is the Word of God. That's why Paul wrote, "... *let God be found true, though every man be found a liar...*" (Romans 3:4, NASB). If your experience and logic tell you one thing, but the Word of God says something else, go with the Word. You can't trust your experience or your limited, human reasoning.

This is the very area in which so many Christians have a hard time. Someone stands in a healing line for prayer and, for whatever reason, doesn't see the manifestation of their healing. Based on their experience, they draw a conclusion: *Healing isn't for me. I know God heals some people, but He must not heal everyone, because I didn't get healed.* On the surface, this sounds like a logical conclusion based on experience. There is, however, a problem with this; it is contrary to the Word of God.

First Peter 2:24 says, "[Jesus,] *Who his own self bare our sins in his own body on the tree, that we, being dead to sins, should live unto righteousness: by whose stripes ye were healed.*" Matthew 12:15 tells us, "*...and he [Jesus] healed them all.*" Every day you will be faced with the decision to either go with what your experience and senses tell you, or with what the Word says about a given situation. Therefore, make a decision not to allow strongholds to be erected in your life.

Religion and False Doctrine

There is a third common source of wrong thinking. Ironically, people often get infected with this kind right inside the walls of their local church. I'm talking about concepts and ideas that spring from religious traditions and false teachings.

Much of what is communicated and emphasized in religious circles today has absolutely nothing to do with the truth of God's Word. That shouldn't come as a big surprise, because the same thing was true in Jesus' day. He was God incarnate— a living, breathing representation of God's nature and will; yet, He was constantly in trouble with religious leaders who were supposedly dedicated to serving God.

How could that be? Jesus Himself exposed the nature of the problem. Somewhere along the way, religious tradition had become more important than the truth of God's Word and His ways. In one encounter with the Pharisees, Jesus laid it on the line and told them, *"…And by this you invalidated the word of God for the sake of your tradition. You hypocrites, rightly did Isaiah prophesy of you: 'This people honors me with their lips, but their heart is far away from me'"* (Matthew 15:6-8, NASB).

Jesus delivered a similar message on another occasion. In Mark 7:13, He told a group of religious leaders that they were making the Word of God of no effect through their traditions and other things they did. Did you catch that? Jesus told them they had managed to make the mighty, powerful, creative Word of God ineffective through their religious traditions. Strongholds of religious tradition and false teaching will do the same thing in your life. That's why it is so imperative that you contrast everything you hear against the standard of God's Word, including what you're reading in this book right now.

Paul praised the Christians at Berea, because they were open to the things of God while still being vigilant to check everything against the standard of the Word. He said, *"Now these were more noble-minded than those in Thessalonica, for they received the word with great eagerness, examining the Scriptures daily to see whether these things were so"* (Acts 17:11, NASB). Just because a man with degrees or a title says something doesn't make it so. God's Word encourages us to test everything.

Take a look at Paul's advice to the Colossians: *"Beware lest any man spoil you through philosophy and vain deceit, after the tradition of men, after the rudiments of the world, and not after Christ"* (Colossians 2:8). False teaching will spoil you. To *spoil* means to "make rotten or corrupt." How does this happen? False church doctrines and teaching can shape your patterns of thinking in ways that make it difficult or impossible for you to operate in the anointing.

There are entire denominations that experienced the power and presence of God at one time in their history. Now nothing remains but form and tradition. Their traditions have made the Word unproductive. Other segments of Christianity will tell you that God doesn't heal anymore; yet in Exodus 15:26, God says, *"…I am the Lord that healeth thee."*

Others will tell you that the spiritual offices of apostles or prophets passed away in the first century. Yet Ephesians 4:11-13 tells us that these offices will remain until we all come together in the unity of the faith and have attained the full stature of Jesus:

And he gave some, apostles; and some, prophets; and some, evangelists; and some, pastors and teachers; For the perfecting of the saints, for the work of the ministry, for the edifying of the body of Christ: Till we all come in the unity of the faith, and of the knowledge of the Son of God, unto a perfect man, unto the measure of the stature of the fulness of Christ....

I could cite example after example, but the point is that if you allow unbiblical religious teachings to sink into your thinking, they will rob you of faith and confidence where these matters are concerned. You will miss out on the power and blessing that God has made available to you, because you won't have any faith or expectation to receive them.

It shouldn't come as a surprise to discover that Christians who have been wrongly taught that God doesn't want them to prosper aren't experiencing very much prosperity. Believers who have been taught that healing passed away with the last apostle aren't healed very often. Again, these are strongholds—deeply entrenched deceptions that spring from religious tradition and false doctrine.

To be *forewarned* is to be armed beforehand. Now that you know where the seeds of strongholds are likely to come from, you can be on guard and keep them from ever being planted. Therefore, make sure that you are not absorbing unbiblical thoughts and ideas from the world, your own experiences and conclusions, or religious tradition. If you will rightly divide the Word of God and compare every thought and attitude with it, you will remain free of strongholds and the destructive consequences they bring.

CHAPTER ELEVEN

Becoming a Person of Discipline

Diligence. *Slothfulness. Lasciviousness. Strongholds.* These are terms that we have examined throughout this book. Each has shown us a different aspect of what is involved in becoming a person of discipline. Disciplined people are those who control their appetites rather than allowing their appetites to control them. They are people who know how to retain control of their bodies. First Thessalonians 4:4-5 (NASB) says, "*...that each of you know how to possess his own vessel in sanctification and honor, not in lustful passion, like the Gentiles who do not know God.*"

According to Colossians 2:5 (NASB), disciplined people gave Paul joy: "*For even though I am absent in body, nevertheless I am with you in spirit, rejoicing to see your good discipline and the stability of your faith in Christ.*" Discipline and stability of faith go together. As you become a more disciplined person, you'll find that your faith is becoming stronger and more effective.

You will also find yourself becoming bolder, less fearful and less timid. Remember what Paul said to Timothy: "*For God has not given us a spirit of timidity, but of power and love and discipline*" (2 Timothy 1:7, NASB). This is a verse on which you should stand and meditate. Receive its promise by faith and allow the spirit of discipline given to you by God to affect your life.

I hope you realize by now that discipline is not a dirty word; it is a biblical one. Being disciplined isn't imprisonment, but freedom from slavery to your appetites; it is freedom from bondage to sin, guilt, shame and self-hatred. Disciplined Christians are the freest people in the world!

There is an anointing of discipline to remove the burdens of lasciviousness and destroy the yokes of strongholds. You will experience the effects of the anointing as you press toward living for Christ, the Anointed One.

As I have stated many times throughout this book, when it comes to basics, becoming a person of discipline and being diligent is all about filling yourself with Jesus. As you fill your mind, heart and mouth with the Word and spend time fellowshipping with Him, you will gradually be transformed into His image through the renewing of your mind. You will be freed from your old cravings, bondages and habits. While on earth, Jesus demonstrated that He is a person of extraordinary discipline. As you become more like Him, you will become disciplined, too.

Jesus wants you to be free. True freedom, however, can only come as you learn to overcome the weaknesses of your flesh and resist the enemy's attempts to re-enslave you. Consider what Galatians 5:1 (NASB) says: "It was for freedom that Christ set us free; therefore keep standing firm and do not be subject again to a yoke of slavery." Keep standing firm, because Jesus, the Anointed One and His Anointing, has set you free!

Five Steps to Complete Salvation

1. Recognize and admit that you are a sinner (Psalm 51:5).

2. Repent of your sins (1 John 1:9).

3. Confess Jesus Christ as your Lord and Savior (Romans 10:9-10).

   "Father, in the name of Jesus, I recognize and admit that I am a sinner. I repent of my sins, making a 180 degree turn away from them toward You by changing my heart, mind and direction. I confess with my mouth that Jesus is Lord, and I believe in my heart that You raised Him from the dead. I invite You to come into my life, Lord Jesus, and I thank You that I am saved. Amen."

4. Receive baptism by water (Matthew 3:6) and the Baptism of the Holy Spirit with the evidence of speaking in tongues (Acts 2:3-4, 38; Acts 8:14-17).

5. Pray, read and obey the Word of God daily (Joshua 1:8; Proverbs 4:20-23; 1 John 5:3).

Keys to Receiving the
Baptism of the Holy Spirit

1. Understand that the Holy Spirit was poured out on the day of Pentecost (Acts 2:1-4).

2. Remember that salvation is the only qualification necessary for receiving the Baptism of the Holy Spirit (Acts 2:38).

3. Know that the laying on of hands is scriptural (Acts 8:17; Acts 19:6).

4. Dispel all fears about receiving a counterfeit spirit (Luke 11:11-13).

5. Open your mouth as an act of faith to receive the Holy Spirit (Ephesians 5:18-19).

About the Author

Dr. Creflo A. Dollar is the pastor and founder of the 25,000-member World Changers Church International, a non-denominational church located in College Park, Georgia.

Dr. Dollar received the vision for World Changers Ministries (WCM) in 1981 while a student at West Georgia College. God instructed him to teach the body of Christ the Word of God with simplicity and understanding. In February of 1986, WCM held its first worship service with only eight members at Kathleen Mitchell Elementary School in College Park. Attendance grew rapidly, and as a result, the ministry relocated to a modest-sized chapel, then later moved to its present location—the 8,500-seat sanctuary called the World Dome.

A world-renowned author, Dr. Dollar has written several books on a variety of topics, including debt-cancellation, healing, prosperity, prayer and victorious living. Many of his past works, including *Understanding God's Purpose for the Anointing* and *The Divine Order of Faith*, have been added to the curriculum of several Christian colleges across the United States.

Dr. Dollar received his Doctorate from Oral Roberts University in 1998 and serves on the Board of Regents. In addition to being a successful businessman and entrepreneur, he is also the publisher of *Changing Your World* Magazine, an inspirational publication.

If You Would Like:

- To order books and tapes by Dr. Creflo A. Dollar
- To become a partner or supporter of Creflo Dollar Ministries
- To become an e-mail subscriber and receive the latest information concerning ministry events, new releases and special offers
- To receive a FREE subscription to the *Changing Your World* Magazine

Call Us:

United States and Canada . . . .(866) 477-7683
United Kingdom . . . .+44-121-359-5050
Australia . . . .+61-7-5528-1144
South Africa . . . .+27-11-792-5562
West Africa . . . .+234-1-270-5438

Or visit our Web site:

www.creflodollarministries.org